Seven Hours at the Ocean

By

Ty Davis

1

Seven Hours at the Ocean 2012

To the memory of my daughter, Beth.

Death doesn't change the way we love,

only the way we touch.

There are families and then there are "those families" – the ones in which a child, a brother, a sister, a wife or a husband has died first.

I am a member of one of "those families."

It has been ten years since the death of my daughter, Beth.   These years were filled with two events: Not wanting to remember and fearing that I wouldn't remember enough. Mixed in were nights of tears, "what if" thinking, "if only" bargaining, and endless, endless hours of missing her in our lives - from holidays, to graduations, to birthdays, to weddings, to just the every days.

In looking back, I know one truth: I endured time. There is this belief that time heals all wounds. It is a lie because the heart does not know time.

I once read that the loss of a child is called "eternity's sorrow." I accept that I will carry this sorrow, this pain, for the rest of my life. But what I don't accept is that I must become this pain. And so, I made a bargain with God or the Creator, that for one week – seven days – I would go to the ocean to sit for one hour. I chose the ocean because my Comanche father once told me that the ocean was the Mother of All Life. Perhaps, if I listened, I may see or hear of a new life, not one that endures pain, but one that becomes more because of it.

What follows is what was given.

Day One, First Hour

    I drive the ten miles for my first hour at the ocean. I brought fear along. I hate fear - not for what it is - but for what it does to me. I feel small and insignificant and unable to cope. This time, the fear comes from a nightmare; a dream that felt so real, I woke up gasping for breath. Even though the dream is over, the fear remains, my legs are wobbly and my hands are shaking. I pull into the parking lot overlooking Bastendorff Beach. I cut the engine and look out on the gray-blue day.

    It's 10:22 in the morning.

    I see a mother and daughter. The girl is carrying a white plastic sword. As they walk, the girl is stabbing kelp and sand and logs. Both are bundled up; heavy coats, hats, boots, gloves. I look to the outside temperature gauge. It is 45 degrees. A light wind is coming from the south, and it feels odd because it is cold. Usually,

southerlies are warm. Clouds fill the sky, some
smooth, others with big puffs of gray and darker gray.
The ocean is a sea of white waves, rumbling in a
haphazard tumble onto the sand. It is almost high
tide. As the water goes back out, it leaves a mirrored
gray sheen on the sand.

Rain starts to beat against the windshield, making
it impossible to see out. I turn on the ignition so
that I can turn on the wipers. Between swipes, I see
the mother and daughter as they reach their older car.
It has a few dents and the green paint has faded. I
wave and the mom smiles, waves back while the little
girl gets in the back seat. They leave with the
little girl watching me, the sword held straight up.
I am alone at the beach on a spring day that is
anything but winter in disguise. It looks like my fear
and I long for a white plastic sword.

I look out over the ocean and see the wind bend
beach grass, grass that is full of errant raindrops,
the ones which refuse to completely fall to the
ground. More storm clouds do a fast dance across the

orizon. It makes me dizzy - as if I am moving as
well. There are days like that, where the world is
spinning too fast, and I, the reluctant traveler, fear
that I will spin off into the sky. I roll down the
window just to smell the ocean, to ground me. I am hit
not only with the smell of the ocean, but of the sand,
kelp and beach grass. I become settled.

Seagulls fly by with a few crows in tow. I
love the crows; not so much the seagulls. Crows
seem less greedy, more intelligent. This may just
be my perception though, not one based on reality.
Animals and birds do what they need to do to
survive - just like humans. It just isn't always
fairly done.

I look around the inside of the car. I have
an old quesadilla and some stale bread that I can
feed the birds. I know all the arguments about how
bad it is to feed wildlife, but I can't have
unwanted food go to waste when another is hungry.
I throw bits out and one crow sees me, only to
"caw, caw, caw!" to the others, and soon, there

are twenty-or-so others flying around and landing by my car. They keep their distance, rushing in for food only to rush out. A crow grabs a big piece - one that he can't eat all at once. The others chase him as he tries to hop away, all cawing and cawing. He takes off and the others follow, trying to swoop down on him, take the food. I can't tell if he got away with it.

I throw more of the quesadilla out. A seagull notices and calls to the others. His call is different and sounds more like a scream. Soon the sky is full of white and black wings against the gray clouds. It is beautiful and yet sad. All this movement for what little food is on the sand. I feel guilty that I am not feeding them the right food and what I did bring can't possibly feed them all; today only the greedy and brave eat.

I look for the pelicans. They rarely travel alone, and if you are lucky, you come across them as they feed. Flying low they swoop up only to nose dive, wings tucked in perfect form, only to hit the water hard with a splash that rivals a belly flop. A couple of days ago when I was out here, a single pelican walked by my car. I thought it was odd that it came up to me and I remember thinking, "This is the most awesome thing ever, and oh my god, do they bite?!" It was beautiful and I moved away – more from fear than from anything the bird was doing – jumping back into my car. I had crackers and pears and cheese, and I tried to share, but nothing would fall into that incredible beak; it opened and closed as I tossed the food, but it all bounced off and landed in the sand. The pelican soon walked away, and I truly felt like I disappointed the bird. It was as if I was the first to meet an alien and when asked for wisdom, I offered up crackers and pears and cheese. But mainly it was about its beauty - and how I moved away from it. It had been so long that I had experienced beauty, that when given, I didn't know how to react or receive.

Instead, I hear a meadowlark. It is the bird of my childhood, and its song makes me smile. I remember the Wyoming mornings, clear blue skies and a sun that knows its way. Here, in Oregon, the skies are rarely blue: grays and greens are the dominant colors mixed in with cold rain or colder rain. I am instantly homesick. Wyoming has my heart, always will.

It's 10:28.

I sit, not trusting my legs. Fear has its grip. I look out over the ocean and see nothing but water and clouds. If you stare long enough, you can get lost in that view, similar to looking at a plain white wall. Eventually, you forget where it begins and ends. Two crows swoop over the car, they are fighting over something. They land in front of me only to be met by a third that tries but isn't able to steal the something. The two remain as the loser flies off. A seagull flies overhead so close that I swear I can feel what it is like to fly.

I want to fly.

I turn on the radio. Is that allowed? Benny and the Jets come on and the two crows start strutting to the music. I have seen humans dance like that. I turn it off and the crows fly away.

A white truck pulls into the parking lot; a man and a woman are inside. The man gets out with a beagle and they both walk away heading north, leaving the woman in the truck. She is writing on a notepad, like she is making a list and she doesn't look up. The steps he takes are marked in the wet sand, steps that seem to be following along. With time, the wind or the rain will take them all away.

I look to the south and notice logs out on the sand. They look like seals and whales. Sometimes I wonder about nature, about how nature mimics us. Or is it the other way around?

It's 10:49.

The man and his beagle coming back and I watch him as he walks with his dog. He does a bit of a jig, playing with the dog. I laugh. They walk up to their truck and the dog waits by the door to get in. Leash off, jump in and the dog licks the sand off his legs. This is a familiar routine for the dog. The man waves to me and they leave. The woman never looks up from her list.

I am alone again.

The sky is lightening to a whiter gray. The rain has stopped and I see traces of blue mixed between the clouds. The sand is taking on the color of the sky again. An old green truck drives up. It feels like an invasion. I like being alone in this moment, lost to what I see and feel.

A heavy-set man gets out and looks at the ocean. I think nothing of him - just another guy at the beach. He has on an old coat and hat that seems like it's an old work hat, it says, "Gone Fishin'." He opens the back door and gets out a green plastic bucket with a couple of plastic shovels. The man picks something up from the front and puts it beside the truck. It's then I notice the feet, little ones, belonging to a little guy, about two years old. The boy points to the beach and the man nods as he reaches for his hand. Instead, the little boy grabs a finger. The man shifts his hold and you can tell it's familiar: It's how they hold hands. I watch as they walk away; the man with the plastic pail and shovels, and the little boy watching the sea.

And then this man that I initially thought nothing of brings a memory forward – of a time when I brought my kids to the beach for the first time:

They flew in from Wyoming. I was divorced and living in Oregon, attending law school. Three years earlier, the Wyoming judge hearing our custody battle, fell asleep during the hearing, called me a "wounded

knee" and awarded custody of my kids to their
father. It took a law degree to get them
back. They came out after my first year of
law school. We drove to Cannon Beach and I
remember them getting out of the car. They
all three paused for a second, looked at me,
looked at the ocean, and took off leaving my
youngest son and husband at the car. We
caught up with them as they made it back from
touching the water. It was cold, cold, cold
and the northerly added to it all, but their
eyes were alive. I felt like I had showed
them a treasure. Beth made sand castles and
talked on and on and her brothers called her
"Babbles."

I smile with the memory and then cry,
hard. Memories usually bring joy. Mine bring
more pain. Most likely because these memories
are all I will have with Beth - nothing more.
Her brothers have gone to having children and
new worlds and experiences. Beth is frozen in

time and time is constantly moving away from
her.

It's 11:08.

My eyes hurt and I feel a migraine coming
on. I look for a rainbow because they are another
memory. Rainbows bring Johnny Mo's wishes, his
mother said. Johnny Mo was killed in the 1990's
and his mother is a friend. He was my second love.
He visits me in dreams, teaching me about the
feeling of joy. I am a hard learner, it seems. No
rainbows today, but Johnny Mo is still around me.
How many rainbows have I missed? I'll have to send
a note on to his mother. His birthday is May 16
and I make sure I remember it, honoring her and
Johnny Mo - for all of us.

It seems as if I am remembering a lot of
memories today. It wasn't my intent, but it must
be the way; moving forward by understanding your
beginnings. Indians say you have to know your

beginnings in order to understand where you are going. I didn't understand that until today.

The sun comes out. I think it must be a quick-change artist, dashing between clouds in an eight-part play. The gray clouds open to expose a vivid blue, then the clouds come together again and it all goes back to the gray. It does this again and again – clouds dancing with the sun.

I see seagulls out on the sand waiting for food. This place, the world of the ocean, looks peaceful. Peace. I long for peace. "And then what?" I hear. It is a whisper.

I don't know.

The crows fly by again and land in front of me. They walk and then pick at the ground only to feed off of pieces of straw. I grab the bread, and throw more out, trying to reach the crows. They see it but won't come any closer to the car.

They are patient.

I look out over the beach and I see the little boy again. Still holding the man's finger, they have moved out from behind a small sand dune. They haven't gone very far - maybe 100 feet. The man is still looking at the ocean. He might be a fisherman. He has the haunted look of loving the ocean but having to live on the dirt. The boy looks like he is treasure hunting - picking up bits of shells and rocks and wood and putting them in the bucket. It takes time to collect treasures at the ocean. Another patient one.

And then the little boy stops and stares; he is looking at a log, a log with a thousand white and black and gray barnacles. His walk quickens, well, his tottering does. It is hard to walk in sand when you are little and trying to place your green alligator boots just so. He gets to the log and bends over as if resting. Patting the log, he swings a leg over, crawls on and sits. He moves back and forth as if the log is a horse. Playing horse. I smile and I send thanks to them. They brought another memory - Beth loved her rocking horse when she was two, back and forth, hard and fast.

Gratitude.

I realize that I am sitting on the edge of the world in a place that is full of beauty and magic and wonder. Mix all that in with my memories and pain, and I see that beauty, magic and wonder can maybe heal this pain. Truly, while it is understood that the unseen things like love and forgiveness are important in life, it is the beauty in nature that can lead you to a new world - a world of beginnings.

It is 11:20.

I look out to the ocean and I see two young girls playing out in the surf. They don't have wetsuits on - only swimsuits. The water is about 50 degrees. I can't imagine what they are feeling in that cold water and cold wind. But what I see is pure joy. Joy outside of the cold.

It's time to go. I get out and walk around a bit. I head to a point overlooking the ocean. I pause and wonder when will my steps not hurt so much? Walking back, I think, I can't worry about steps made in the sand.

It is 11:22.

Day Two, Second Hour

I bring irritation to the ocean today. I tried to talk myself out of this bargain I made but none of my reasons seem to rise up over my side of the deal. And so I am here.

It is 10:19 in the morning.

The sky is gray. The clouds are empty of rain. The ocean is a beautiful aqua-blue and I roll down the window only to be immediately overwhelmed by the smells and sounds of life at the beach. The waves are loud, big and mushy. Surfers use the term "mushy," and because I am a kook (novice surfer) I shouldn't, but I do, as if I am in the know. I suppose I do know enough. Mushy means that the waves are backing-off and without form; not good for surfing. The beach break looks like an endless white, with spider webs crossing across the waves. The sun peeks through some lighter clouds giving the sand, ocean

and sky a bit of a yellow softness. Off the
horizon are some bits of blue sky. This lightening
of the sky seems as if the world is a bit lighter,
too. As if the world breathes easier.

I don't feel as if I am part of that world.
I carry too much pain, too much sadness. Sadness
is heavy.

I look to the sand. A couple is out on the
beach walking their dogs. I believe that dogs are
the true friends because they don't pretend their
emotions. Joy is joy, tired is tired, grumpy is
grumpy. The emotions outweigh any of their reasons
and it seems as if that would be enough to get
along in life - if we just told each other how we
felt.

A crow cries out. I brought sunflower seeds
today and I reach over and grab them. I wonder if
they will eat sunflower seeds.

A text comes in. It is from Beth's friend,
Andrea. She sends pictures of her daughter,

Elizabeth, named after Beth, and her son, Alex. It stops me. She has more new life, and I had my life, my daughter, taken from me. One time in my life, I was jealous of life, even the life of a bee, an ant, a flower. How can it be that that this spark of life is absent in my daughter? I don't go there anymore, but I do long for the possibility that my daughter would have, could have been a mother by now - like her friends. When a life is taken, the impact, the ripple is forever. Whatever immortality she could have given to the world, is gone. I think about living for Beth. Could I be her immortality? What would she do today?

She would say, "Come on, Momma," and grab my hand, pulling me out onto to the beach. I wish she was here. I could lean on her as I walk. But today, alone, I sit in the car. My legs don't seem to want to do anything anymore.

I see the log from yesterday. The barnacles are whiter in the sun - barnacles that once found a home on the wood. This log, once a seed, grew to a tree, only to die in order to be used for some man-made function, then to be lost at sea, to be washed ashore, to end up on this beach, and to be a pretend horse to a little boy. How many changes in its world. How many gifts. And even now, lying on the beach, dead, it adds beauty. How is it that death adds beauty?

I throw the sunflower seeds and the crows arrive They don't recognize the seeds at first. A hop, another hop, a walk, a fly up, a drop down, a hop. One comes closer and pecks at the seeds and then a call to the others. The brave ones, the hungrier ones get the food first. Always and again. About 20 sit back and watch. I am part of that 20 today.

A woman with a white dog, a bichon, I think, walks by. The dog is short to the ground and its muzzle full of fur almost sweeps the sand. I smile. She steps on the seeds - she doesn't see them. I react and then let go. She didn't know that she was stepping on a gift, on food for the birds. I wonder if she has a life that has not been shattered by sudden death. Where your goodbyes are left for you, and you alone. Spoken in the night.

Beth died in the night. It was fast and furious on the back of a motorcycle. The driver, her friend, was drunk. He missed a turn; she hit the guardrail with her head. Instant. No pain, they said. But they were wrong. I know she knew. She saw it coming and that is pain. I lived her death a thousand times. That moment when she knew it was coming. It steals my breath, my heart, my life. Even now.

Her friend lived. Broke his shoulder, went to jail for 90 days for being criminally negligent in causing a death. I talked with him a year later. I gave him permission to have a good life - a life Beth would want to live, to be more to his family, his daughter. To live.

Forgiveness.

I look away from my heart to see what I can see out over the ocean.

It's 10:24.

A grandmother walks by with two grandsons. Yellow buckets in hand. No shovels. No handholding. They go off down the beach. I think of the innocence of holding hands. It means so much and is so simple of an act. I think of Beth's hands. She drew them once and I still have the drawings. I study them just as I did when she was alive. She fascinated me. Where did she get what is Beth - her looks, that laugh, her hair, her eyes? I am grateful that I took the time to see her, to watch her.

Odd I am here, watching, now. Alone. I used to hate the ocean. Everywhere you step, something is alive - sand fleas, kelp, crabs, moss, and fish. It was overwhelming to a mountain girl. To a girl that wouldn't kill an ant.

But now, it is a place where I can touch the earth. There are no expectations of me, no relationships to worry about, no obligations. Just the ocean and me. I love the ocean. It took 20 years to say that, to appreciate such a foreign place. I am taking the time to watch it, I think. And I notice where I step - even trying to avoid the millions of sand fleas for their sake and mine.

Off to the south is a rock out-cropping. There is a hole in the rocks, and it is visible today in between waves. I want to paint that place, the south end of Bastendorff Beach.

A crow drops down on a tire rut and almost tumbles over. He recovers and struts away. Off to the left of me, the 20 crows are still watching the seeds. We take crows for granted. They have a complex social existence. They mate for life. They are the curious to me.

My son calls. He asks why I am here. I give a small answer – not the one I am feeling. Later. He can read it and then understand.

A young man walks by out near the surf. I think he looks like a romantic. I imagine him the suffering artist walking through a problem on the beach.

I worry that I won't understand this hour.

A car drives up. A grandmother gets out. She is dressed in black but for her red boots. Her granddaughters, one in a pink coat and another in a red coat, get out. I wonder if she is a widow. She acts sad, her shoulders are hunched, and her face is lined with what looks to be worry. She doesn't smile. They take off. Pink Coat runs ahead and bends down to touch the kelp, the log, the beach grass. She dashes to the right and then to the left. She picks up two sticks and puts them on her head like antennae. Rushing back to her grandmother, she is smiling, but her grandmother doesn't notice.

"I see," I whisper.

The sun breaks through, the yellow light becomes more intense and the white of the waves become brilliant. I think about the word, "aware." Is it better to be aware or not? Is it better to be aware of pain and loss or not. If I could, would I choose to forget my daughter's death? I know the answer. No. I was with her in the beginning and I will be with her in the end. Regardless of how it ended.

To be aware is to suffer.

I look out. Tears are falling again. I don't wipe them away. I don't have to hide tears here at the ocean.

I see a crow hop closer to my car. Others follow. He hops back and the others follow. It is like a dance of trust. Whose eyes do you trust, yours or the others?

Mine.

A dog runs by - another beagle. He stops and smells the sand, heads over to some rocks, noses them and then eats something that seems wrong. He looks up, turns to see his people, and runs back. They throw a ball and he chases it. No big deal. Eat a bit of something from the beach and then go chase a ball. No worries. La-di-dah.

An American-built car drives up. I can hear a yapper in the back seat. Well, what's left of the yapper's ability to yap. His voice has been intentionally quieted; people do that to their dogs so they can't bark. But this one is able to rasp like an old smoker. A man gets out. He has on a blue sweatshirt and a dog toy in his back pocket. The dog jumps out. It's a black schnauzer. A woman gets out. She is irritated and yells something at the man. He doesn't say anything. I see his big gold necklace around the back of his neck. She goes around the car and stands by him. She has on huge water socks - too big, looking like munchkin shoes. They turn and head south. She waddles behind him and the dog.

The woman and the bichon come back. They walk by and don't notice me. A huge truck with a huge dog drives by us. They look at the beach and leave. The woman and the bichon get in their car and leave.

It is warmer now, the wind is mild, the sun is light and soft and the twenty crows are still worrying the seeds.

It's 11:06.

I get out of my car. I hear the crow's wings as they fly away. I look around me. There is trash all over the parking lot. I start picking it up. I don't understand littering. Never have. Tomorrow, I'll bring a trash bag. There are days where walking with rubber legs is just too much. Maybe, with a purpose, I won't notice my weakness.

How do you explain grief to another? The type of grief that lives in your stomach, your

soul, that takes your strength, makes you afraid
that you will collapse on the world and never
return. Where any strength you may have comes
from fighting to breathe and not living. How do
you explain a world where you have cried so much,
you have no more tears? And yet you cry. Still.

I hear the meadowlark. Again. Day two. This
time, I listen as I used to listen when I was a
girl. Memories do that. They come again and again.
Like waves. I need to hear this again, I think, to
hear the message. The meadowlark's song is beauty.

"Remember me," he sings.

And then it comes to me. With the seagull's
call, the crow's dance, a bit of sun and the
meadowlark's song, perhaps, *perhaps*, I can walk
again if I aim towards beauty. Perhaps I can
become my own safe place; not because I remember
the pain, but because from the pain I am here now.
Love isn't always the light side of life. We think
it is, from teenage crushes to romantic love to

marriages to children and on and on. But the dark side of love - where loss comes in the door - has value if understood. Perhaps, if we understood that, we wouldn't be so quick to walk away from love.

I think of the need to live - the always-hungry in its various forms of greed and envy and wanting - and wonder if there is ever enough life for us all. But then I think that much of our lives are spent living in various forms like that dead tree on the beach, and I intend to leave beauty after I am gone. Time doesn't heal the heart but time can bring the possibility of beauty to eyes that tear up at its possibilities. Even now.

Beauty.

It's 11:19.

Day Three, Third Hour

My hair is long and I wear a warlock, which
is a small braid. It is my symbol that I pray for
strength. I am in a war these days, with my past,
with my present, with my future. I think of this
as I drive up to the ocean.

It is 11:01.

Gibs is with me, he is my husband. It is Sunday
and he promised to disappear for the hour. Even
so, having another here changes the moment. It
just isn't me at the ocean. It is Gibs and me at
the ocean. He gets out as he says goodbye and then
he pauses by the front of the car. I watch as he
looks north then south, and then decision made,
heads south.

Seven cars are here. It is busy. I see trash
and remember I forgot the trash bags. A butterfly
kite spirals down and a girl all in black rolls up
the string. The kite has a pink tail. Another
kite, flown by a girl in lilac boots and coat,

heads north. There is about five knots of wind today. Another cold southerly and the tide is ebbing.

I see Gibs walking on the wet sand. Small waves rush up to meet him. The ocean's tide is always coming in only to pause and then go back out and this movement has been going on for billions upon billions of years.

I look to the beach in front of me. I see a little boy in green boots fall down on his knees to play in the sand. He tries to move the sand to a shape but it is too dry - it needs water. I roll down the window and smell smoke mixed with the smells of the ocean. I think about men and their need for fire. The ancient stories of how fire changed humanity. Two more join Green Boots: Lilac Girl with a green tractor and Camo-Boy. They kneel down and start patting the sand. A fourth, a girl with pink mittens, joins them. A fifth, in a green jacket, shows up with a yellow plastic shovel. It is like a real shovel and he starts to digging in

the sand only to throw the sand on them. They
motion for him to stop and he does, but then holds
the shovel like a weapon, as he watches them play.
He draws it back only to stop. He watches the
mound grow and then jumps on it and stomps it into
nothing. The others ignore him and start over
again. He stops, watches, and starts digging the
sand only to throw it on them. Again.

Two surfers head out, both with shortboards and
I can see the wax on the boards. The waves have
more form today, but it still looks to be a mess
out there. They walk into the water up to their
chests and then hop on their boards. A Coast Guard
helicopter flies by. A fishing boat is off to the
north.

It's 11:17.

I look south. I don't see Gibs. This looking.
It changes this hour. Not because I am not
watching but because I am looking. There is a

difference. Watching is without wanting. Looking is needing something or someone.

The last ten years I have been looking for Beth.

I turn away. A woman with a leopard print hat walks by the car. She is breathless and I can tell she was, or is, a smoker: lines all over her face. She opens her car door. I can smell the smoke. I don't understand smoking. Tobacco for healing and ceremony is different than tobacco for the high, a high that turns into an ugly addiction. I watch her leave, painted fingernails on the steering wheel, matching lipstick and tinted hair. She is a painted lady.

I look south. I can see Gibs by the rocky bluffs. Good. Safe.

I look back to the kids. They have another mound built. Green Jacket is standing, ready to strike. I know about the opposites - the ones that teach you the lessons that you never knew you needed to learn - the law of good versus evil, heaven versus hell, up versus down. Green Jacket picks up kelp and cracks it like a whip. They all get up and run to the ocean, leaving Pink Mittens behind. Green Jacket stomps on the mound and Pink Mittens gets up and follows the others. Children seem to be better at forgiving.

The ocean is roaring. It is the audience to our world today.

Two dogs and three people walk up to the kids. Their kids. They head back to their cars but before they leave, I want to look in Green Jacket's eyes. He walks by and I catch them. They look like the eyes of a seagull.

It's 11:25.

A crow shows up by my door. He caws three times. Another shows up. They caw three times and then two more show up. A woman in red walks by and they all fly away. A silver car drives up with loud techno music.

"You've got to be kidding me," I said to myself. I roll down my window. "Are you leaving that on?" I asked. I feel like an old lady at the beach. The passenger turns it down. He said sorry and they get out their skim boards, one spits on the sand, and they leave - throwing cigarette butts by their car. I get out and go get the butts and put them on their car - but the wind blows them off. Crap. I pick them up and do the trash pickup in the parking lot. There are socks, underwear, candy wrappers, beer cans, a tampon, soda cans, and some things I don't know what they are. I leave the tampon.

I find more cigarette butts. I know what cigarettes do - they steal your air. I watched my step-dad die from smoking; struggling for air as if breathing through a straw. When you are young, that type of tomorrow is so far away, it has no reality. I watched reality kick my step-dad's butt, and smoking is dumb, dumb, dumb.

I see Gibs coming back. It's too early. And there are too many people here today. They crowd the peace and beauty of the ocean. Or maybe not. There's enough room for us all - we just have different ways of experiencing this world. I need to practice patience with others - not just myself.

A girl walks by with hair like my daughters. It takes my breath. I have some of my daughter's hair. Even after ten years, it is still beautiful. I think this might be creepy and I don't tell people about it. Well, until now.

I look at the south-end rock outcroppings. I remember that I want to paint them. They are my focus point, my place in which to catch my bearings. If they are there, then I am here. Simple.

It's 11:42.

I get out again. This time I walk to the oceans edge. I head south then head north then back again. It is cold going south. People walk by with their dogs and wives, husbands and kids. Here, there is nothing but what is here now.

Simplicity.

The ocean is freedom. I give it my memories today because I know of its endless movement – billions upon billions of years of coming in only to pause and go back out. I can understand opposites and I can practice patience.

I can do that.

Simple.

It is 12:01

Day Four, Fourth Hour

My thoughts are of the 100th floor as I drive up to the ocean today. The 100th floor is the place where all the bad things of the world exist:

deaths, hunger, diseases, pain, grief and sadness. Those who have been shattered by these bad things go there when more bad things happen. It isn't a willing trip. It is something that just happens. We blink in response to the bad and we are on the 100th floor.

I am here at the ocean.

It's 10:19.

No one is here today – no cars, no people, no dogs on the beach. One crow flies over to my car and sits on a sand hill, cocking its head back and forth. I look out over the ocean as I roll down the window. The familiar roar, the familiar smell. There is a mist to the day, leaving a million beads of water on my windshield, that eventually form small rivers down the glass. The beach is a mess - the sand full of imprints with bits of wood, kelp and hundreds of rocks of various sizes lying above the high water line. But where the tide has gone, the sand is clean.

A maroon car drives up and then leaves.
Alone. It feels beyond lonely. I think about all
the things we fill our lives up with in order to
avoid feeling lonely. But these things are just
masks. Lonely can only be covered up for so long.
I like being alone and wonder if it is the same
thing.

I look out to the ocean. It is a mess, too.
There is no reason to its surf, haphazard waves
moving and rolling into each other only to fall
away. I imagine, though, that this day, with the
tide, swell and winds, the ocean is just as it
should be. A zipper wave screams by. I love them.
They only occur in the right conditions and it is
an ending wave on the beach that zips
horizontally. My son showed me that a couple of
years ago. I think of how I believe that as a
parent, I show him the world. It isn't true. My
kid's eyes have opened my eyes to the world. I
haven't always been willing, but since Beth
passed, I have been aware of my limitations.

It is gray out: gray sky and gray ocean. The surf has a tinge of gray on the gray sand. It is a monochromatic gray. Crows are eating at the high tide line. I think of how the ocean eventually claims all that is left on the beach. The beach grass is quiet today, heavy with rain. The meadowlark is singing a morning song. I smile. I seem to be familiar to this world now. After only three days, I feel as if I am home. Or maybe not. Maybe it is just a perception wanting reality. Another mask to the lonely. I hope not. I like it here.

I look at the parking lot. Not too bad today, only pink silly string.

It is 10:22.

A man walks by wearing a hooded blue coat. Here, he won't be misinterpreted for danger. I think of the recent events of a young man shot because he looked dangerous; he had on a hooded black coat. As if what we wear makes our heart's dangerous. Weapons don't live in our hearts.

I look to the ocean again. About 20 feet from the shore, the waves are big. They rise only to fall down and roll onto the beach. What they give to the sand is anything but what they were there out on the ocean and I wonder about people, how mobs become more than their individual hate; how they are anything but what they are, alone.

It is 10:27.

I look to the north and can barely see the channel marker. It is just to the left and south of the jetty's entrance. At one time, Coos Bay was a bustling port where tall-ships were built, and there is an abundance of shipwrecks on these shores. The jetty is made of huge rocks and on big swell days, huge rollers come in and batter the rocks. It is a constant, constant movement. Eventually the rocks will erode into sand and the jetty will have to have new rocks.

I am the sand. I was once a rock.

The ocean is cold and unforgiving. Gibs'
brother died in the ocean. It has taken him over
30 years to find peace with this water. He says
this but I can see his soul in his eyes. There is
no peace there. I think he comes here because I do
and he wants to do for me, make me happy, be a
part of my life.

Love with a bittersweet edge.

I am alone today. With my thoughts, which on
a bad day rival the Boogeyman. I can scare myself.
This pain scares me. This grief. This loss. I
don't know how to ease their grips on my heart and
soul. I don't know how to live with pain that has
no ending, grief that comes in waves, some as if a
tsunami, loss that takes and takes. And no one
seems to know how to help me. Counselors,
doctors, and friends - none have answers that I
can hold onto, none that ease the pain, grief and
loss. I know I am not alone, but the ones that

want to go there, to find a way to break it all, are rare. I have a friend in California that knows, but we don't see each other very often. Johnny Mo's mother is another, but she lives in Wyoming. When they call, I feel as if I am a shipwrecked survivor, grasping to leave this island only to be told that there is no room for me on the ship.

And so I watch. My bargain.

The ocean is different today. It is so cold it feels like snow. It happens here every year for a day or so. I love snow, how it smells, tastes, looks in the sun. It is a childhood memory that is easy to carry. It is a memory of a time when I was living - before Beth died.

I look down. I am worrying my hands. I do that. It is a comfort measure, they say. I've always done it. Perhaps so. Some fingers are bent with the worrying, twisted to the side.

I look up and off to the south of me, I see
Scotch Broom, a noxious-smelling bush. It is a
nasty, invasive species. But then, aren't we all.

It is 10:33.

Seagulls huddle down by a small river that
flows into the ocean. I don't know the name of the
creek and I realize I don't know much about this
beach. All I do know is it is named after the
Bastendorff family. I tend to name things anyway,
I mean, names are for convenient reference and I
imagine that if all the birds, insects, trees,
animals, rocks could talk they would have quite
different names than what humans have given them.
The Bastendorff family still lives in the area,
their dairy farm just down the road. Bastendorff
Beach stretches from the rocky bluffs at the south
end to the jetty at the north end. It is about one
mile of flat, sandy beach reaching up to dunes of
beach grass. It is the perfect beach to walk.

I am lost today. My stomach hurts and I
worry about life. I am told that worry is a bad
habit. It is probably true but I haven't gotten to
the depth of my pain. I think that if I do,
perhaps the worry will ease. I don't know if I
ever will get there, though, do you ever get to
the depth of love? Grief is another part of the
dark side of love. A friend told me this so I
can't claim credit to that bit of wisdom. I
question why I am sitting here on a cold misty
April day, next to an ocean that is colder and
more untouchable than what I carry. Because the
ocean will, if given the opportunity, take your
life. Without protection in the north Pacific, one
has a half-their-body weight timeframe (in
minutes) to survive. Boats capsize and rarely does
one live. Grief, on the other hand, is happy to
just take up residence and really won't kill you
unless you forget how to breathe. I can see how
that happens.

I hate this road I am on. I didn't choose this. And if I did, like some people believe, some pre-life choice, I was dumb. Some angel should have stepped in, or a loved one, or God. I didn't need to learn this lesson in this way. My daughter did not have to die so that the ones around her could become better at life. And while her death is not about me, it has become part of my life, not chosen, not wanted, but imposed and heavily carried. Do we take this on when we have children? The possibility that they might die? Do we knowingly expose ourselves to the possibility of this pain? Do we understand that when we sneak into their rooms at night just to make sure they are okay, they are breathing? Do we ever know the consequences of our actions in bringing life into the world? And if we did, would we still choose to have children? And could we ever truly know?

For me. Yes. I would still choose my children. Even now. Because what they bring to my life is more than I could ever have imagined or comprehended. And even though I have one less child, she is continually giving to me from her death, the ability to love even when I have stumbled down the rabbit hole. Love from beyond.

I look up and see myself in the rear view mirror. There is pain on my face. I look in my eyes and see my soul. It looks like a Picasso painting. I hear a whisper, "Handle with care, it is fragile with grief." I am shattered. I know my fragility and know my body is put together with some glue, and if given the right conditions, would erode away. Handle with care. In this world, is that possible?

A seagull swoops over the windshield and lands by my door. Grabbing the bread, I throw some out. He grabs it all, and flies off. This one left nothing behind.

I think of Beth's death. To accept her death would mean to deny her life and I am not ready to do that. That break in reality has not made sense to me because I can still feel her, smell her, and I know that she is with me. Death has changed how I touch – not how I love. I have yet to talk of her in the past tense. She is with me, weaving her love through my life even still. I don't accept her death; I just need to learn how to be with her through death, in her world of existence.

It is 10:40.

A blue car drives up with a lady in a matching blue coat. She is older, wears glasses and sits in her car. She is watching the ocean. I see crows pecking in the sand and I throw out some more bread. But before I do, I tear it into small pieces. If I don't, a seagull will swallow it whole only to get stuck in their throats. And the seagulls always come, even if your intention is to feed only the crows.

A crow from about 200 feet away sees me throw the bread and he flies and caws and drops down. He takes the bread and flies off. I don't know why I marvel at this each time, but I do. Obviously. I write about it. When I was younger, my Comanche father saw me do this once, we were driving to a powwow and I rolled down the window so I could feed the birds. He smiled and said, "Ah, just like your grandmother." I felt proud in that moment, that I was a part of her, even though she died before I was born.

A few more crows drop down and turn to their right side as they edge up to the car. Then they hop sideways closer, closer. As if this makes for an easier escape. I need to learn how to walk sideways. I think about distance and at what point in time are you safe?

The wind picks up from the northwest, the weather is changing. The rain hasn't come yet, and with the light wind, the mist has disappeared. Maybe the rain won't come today, maybe it missed the wind. I wonder about rain and how it is carried along by the wind.

But I have seen rain on crow's backs. Perhaps they carry the rain, too.

It is 10:51.

The Blue Lady leaves. Birds are hanging out around my car. The food is gone, but they stay.

Hope?

The message of the crow:

Eat what is.

Eat what is given.

Fly.

Caw.

Fly.

Look to eat.

Poop.

Carry the rain.

Love until you die.

Fly.

Hope that the lady in the car has food for us.

Fly.

Hop.

Hope.

Is it possible to live a life without feeling the rain? The feathers of birds seem to make it so. Would I choose that existence?

It is 10:57.

The sky is almost blue. I think of the air as God's breath, the rain as God's tears and the ocean as God's soul. I am not religious, for me religion is a road map to spirituality and we all know our spirits. Instead, I just touch the earth in a sacred way because God is present in all things. My Comanche father told me to talk to the rocks: "They listen," he said. "You just have to slow down in order to hear them back."

I am still trying to slow down enough to hear the rocks.

Suddenly, the birds all take to the sky - crows first and then seagulls. They fly high. I don't know why and I search the beach for a reason. I am looking and looking. It makes me antsy. I am the watcher not the looker. And the birds, they have been my friends out here on the edge of the world. They are my world right now. I don't want them to leave me alone, sitting in a car, watching the ocean with a heavy heart.

And then I follow their flight up, up, up and see thousands upon thousands of birds flying high in the sky. There are endless trails of birds, dotting the horizon. Over and over they pass. I look to the south. More! More! I try to take a picture but my camera only sees the sky. I grab my notebook and I draw. And I draw more. So many ways to fly. So many ways to move. I have ten pages of drawings. I feel as if I am inspired, like an old art master who found his muse. I watch

for 30 minutes and I draw. Twenty pages of
drawings! Birds flying in a changing form,
beautiful against the sky. Flying home once again.

My heart has lifted. And then, the magic of
peace walks into my heart. A familiar from long
ago. Is this how life feels?

Gifts. Gifts today.

It is 11:19.

Day Five, Fifth Hour

Trees line the road to Bastendorff Beach, some reaching over to touch each other. The taller and older ones are covered in ivy. New growth falls over the hillside. It is a swirl of green and other greens.

They seem to say, "We have been here and green all winter."

I think of my mother as I pull up to the ocean. My Comanche father left us - my mother, my brother and me - before I was born. She raised us at a time when a white woman with Indian children was seen as "against nature." She was strong then and she is stronger now. Her memories keep her moving. She is still here. She showed us truth when the questions started.

"Why are we different?"

"You aren't."

"But we are. Our skin is different."

"It doesn't matter. We are all the same, even you."

"But we get called names."

"Ignore them. We are all the same, even you."

It is 2:50.

A squirrel is sitting on a rock watching the ocean. A lone person with a small dog is off to the south end. Two other cars are here and an RV is parked further down the road. A fishing boat, outriggers positioned, heads out to sea. The tide is coming in and the ocean has a swirl of green under the gray clouds. There is no blue and there is no sun today. The crows are down on the sand, picking, picking. They don't look my way.

I have some old granola.

I roll down the window and the air smells clean. I don't see rain in the clouds. Two meadowlarks are singing their afternoon song. The ocean is rough as it washes up onto the beach. I watch the fishing boat as it rolls in the ocean's swell; it looks like a teeter-totter. I get seasick just watching it move.

My former boss called. I love talking to him. We worked together for ten years. We built things and we created things. I am a better person, a better lawyer, because of him. We were all 'fired' in 2010. Indian politics uses many words to get rid of people. In the end, out the door is out the door. That is another pain spot. But not for here. I close that memory and look to the ocean.

I love the ocean's voice; it overshadows the incessant voice of humans. I imagine that God tires of our words. What would the world sound like, if just for one minute, we were collectively silent? It comes to me that my words should be chosen wisely because what I say goes to God. What a humbling thought.

I have a migraine today and it changes how I see things. I try to ignore it. I take another Excedrin. But no matter what I do or what I take, the migraine has to run its 36-hour course. I am not alone but that fact doesn't help at this moment. Perhaps later, I can swap stories with the others: We tend to migraine at the same time because it is a weather thing, a stress thing, a food thing, a sensitive thing - if you read the literature on it. I think it is a life-thing and how we move through the world; we are the canaries in the cage in the mine - the first to sense danger.

I look to the north; the jetty rocks are wet, which means high surf. Wet rocks are always a clue if you happen to be walking out on the jetty. Those waves can be deadly. I have watched families walk out on the jetty to watch the waves and worry for their children. I have even warned them, but most look at me like I am Hinny-Penny. I also warn kids that play in the ocean to watch for the rip tide. Rip tides are like rivers in the ocean and have their own current. They can pull you out to sea rather quickly, and unless you know to swim across and not against it - it is a fruitless endeavor to fight it. I think of this as it applies to life. I think I have been fighting the grief current. Corny thought, corny analogy, but it fits. I don't think I was going there with this thought; rather the point is that if you see a rattlesnake lying in the sun, you don't wait for the rattle to warn you - you step away because you know the nature of the snake. That is the point: Know the nature of the ocean.

I sent a picture of the ocean to my son. He moved away last year and lives in a place away from the surf. He would want to know how the ocean looks. When he was young, I worried whether he knew enough about the nature of the ocean to calm my fears. He learned, and he learned with friends.

He surfs beyond my fears and it is a good lesson for me in trust. My other son still lives by the ocean, a warmer one, and he takes surfing to other levels. My children, the teachers teaching the teacher. I am humbled.

I look out over the ocean before me. Someone had a bonfire on the beach last night; singed wood and trash litter the sand. The birds have picked over the place, leaving plastic and cans. I am going to clean that up tomorrow. Not today. The pain keeps me still. Sitting in my car.

Time to feed the birds. I can do that. I wave my arm out the window, and one comes, others following his flight and call. I throw the granola but the weight of it won't let me throw it very far. The crows sit in a circle around my car. They do their crab walk and hop and I watch. It is like watching the same funny scene. You never get tired of it. Well, at least I don't. There is always a new nuance in the movement.

A lady dressed in black walks up with her small dog. He looks like a wiener dog mix, his little legs moving three times for every step she takes. She is heavy and is breathing hard. The crows fly away, safe in the trees east of the cars. She doesn't see me, gets in her car and leaves. The crows come back, surrounding me and they start their calling.

Today, I am the silent one, careful with my words.

A crow flies too close and hits the passenger door. I hate that sound. It has such finality to it. You can't argue with pain or even death. That is a lawyer's nightmare, the lack of argument. I used to dream of Beth right before she died, where I could save her. And then I dreamed of her after she died, but she was still with us and I was wondering if I should tell her she was dead.

I didn't. Save or tell.

I see the RV door open and a man steps out. He walks out on the beach and then turns around to come back. He stops at the door, shaking out the sand from his feet. Sand never leaves. Because it is a freedom runner, it runs into every possible nook and cranny, shoe, and blanket. I wonder where it wants to go and if it knows. Or maybe it is enough just to be free.

People are like sand. They run and get into worlds only to run to new worlds - freedom runners with actual legs - always looking for something. I think of what I wrote before, how a good life is one that aims for beauty. If sand stopped, what beauty would it create? And if created, would it last?

Doubtful.

It is 3:15.

I throw out more granola. The granola nearest my door is untouched and it is also the granola that is thickest. It just won't go very far because its weight makes it more like a kite tail.

The crows aren't coming close. It seems as if I am not to be trusted today. The message is: The crows are waiting for me to leave.

Leave. I can't. The bargain keeps me here. I apologize that they have to wait a bit longer.

I look back to the ocean. It is turning color. The white of the waves remind me of a time when I was looking for luminescence when my friend and I were sailing. Luminescence is microorganisms that live in the ocean. When they are disturbed, they light up like green neon; fireflies in the water. It happens during the algae bloom. While sailing at night, I looked at the water as the rudder cut through it and didn't see anything. I was told to flush the head (that's the toilet on a boat), and I would see the flashes of neon-green as I pumped seawater in the bowl. I did, and I laughed as I

pumped again and again - only to laugh and laugh
more! Takes potty humor to a new light. Neon pee.

I smile and laugh to myself. I miss him.

The ocean is before me and it takes very
little energy to watch her. The clouds are thick
today and I can't tell the cloudy sky from the
ocean, the horizon is gone. You lose perspective
when that happens. I am reading about vanishing
points and perspective. When there is none, the
meaning of the picture becomes off.

My picture is off.

The crows catch my eye. A few brave ones hop
up to my car and grab some food only to be
attacked as they fly away. Humans do that too. We
aren't so different from the animals and it's only
our conscience that separates us by a very fine
hair.

I have thick Indian hair.

The wind is light, and the beach grass is humming rather than singing as it works to part the wind. I have been told I think too much. I think, rather, I see too much. How do you filter a big imagination, or do you even want to? I don't but others do. Like teaching kids to color inside the lines.

I see dandelions ready to seed out in the grass - their yellow long gone. It's only April. I still can't get used to that here on the coast. In Wyoming, you wouldn't see seeded dandelions until July. There is a sense to logical growth in Wyoming because the winters provide the break between growing and not growing. Not here, something is always growing; there is no break.

My head hurts. The pain is over the left side, the evil side that can take me to 12 hours of bathroom duty. A migraine is like having the flu while seasick. There is nothing you can do but ride it out. And then for days afterwards, recover. I can deal with the pain but not all the other visual and balance and smells - triggers and symptoms that feel as if you have just added the fun house out on the ocean.

And even through all the pain in the world, all the grief, all the darkness, the world keeps turning. I wonder if it ever looks back. Wants to do a "Do Over." Fix the wrongs. Does love conquer all? When Lois Lane died, Superman spun the world backwards so that he could stop the events leading up to her death. That's when you knew he loved her. Up until then, there was just a hint of love.

I wish I was Superman, turn the world backwards for love, to save you, to save me - to save Beth.

When I was a kid, my brother and I played Superman and Superboy and Supergirl and Superdog and Supercat. We all had white capes. He talked me into jumping off the back deck once, saying, "Supergirl could do it!" I still remember that long drop down, more so than the pain when I hit.

Back then, I had things in my life which made me strong: My family, my dog, my horses, my bike, my friends. The moon and stars were my keystones because they are so old; my grandparents parents, and their parents all saw what I am seeing in the night sky - they were what I hung onto in the dark of the night. But here in Oregon, the moon and stars are missing from my sight too often; the Oregon clouds obscure the sky more often than not. I know they are there, and they do the same dance, over and over. After billions of years, they are still there.

So if they are still there, but I can't see them, does that make their presence less?

No, I just need to find a way to see without seeing.

I think of all that grows in the world: plants, animals, and humans. Perhaps they/we are life's reasons - the music, the joy, the love, the beauty, and the magic. And the earth with the sun and the moon and the stars provides the stage in which to make it all possible. If so, I have to learn how to dance a bit better, play a bit better, laugh more, love more, sing more, and grow more.

It is time for more - not the kind that takes - but the kind that gives.

I think of our beginnings. Perhaps we are like the ocean; it is our mother after all. We are given life only to return it much as the ocean moves with its endless cycle. Birth to death to death to birth. Tide in and tide out.

I look out over the ocean. It has made it so difficult to return to her - familiar yet not; warm but not; peaceful but not. We can ride on her, we can swim in her, sail on her, but not live in her. Maybe we aren't meant to return until it is our time. Until then, we are to live.

I think of life before birth, and life after death. If we are to have an understanding of life now, know our beginnings, it is feasible to know of life beyond breath - at either end.

I have talked to a psychic who nailed my daughter's death, words, and mannerisms without any knowledge or cues on my part. I have read books about the After Life. Cynics say I am engaging in comfort measures, that psychics and religion and spiritual mumbo-jumbo are just opiates for the soul.

But I would suggest speaking with a mother or a father - one who has lost a child - and then let's talk about "comfort measures." There is no comfort.

I believe that Beth has found a world that I can't see or touch, but can feel. If I can slow down time, perhaps, like talking to the rocks, I can hear her. It gives me hope and who can fight hope? Hope is like taking hold of a hand, one finger at a time. I am glad that hands have so many fingers. Do we remember the first time we

took a hand? As a baby? Our parents do. They have
been with us since our beginning, and for that, I
am grateful. With the good, the bad, the ugly, we
have been together. That is love, I think.
Staying, maybe not always physically, but with our
hearts. The secret is to understand that. I think
how that might help people who are divorcing or
who are living through a death - love stays, we
carry it, nothing can change that or take it away.
Love is our essence, our breath and helps us aim
for beauty with hope.

The clouds are darkening. Rain is coming. The
wind is picking up and I watch as the waves start
to change. They start out clean and crisp, but the
eight second ride ends and then they fold over
upon themselves in a mess of opaque white.
Seagulls take to the sky; they are the ocean's
wing. They too, are freedom runners.

It is 3:27.

A fishing boat is coming back. Its outriggers are up, but as the boats rolls side to side they still almost touch the ocean. The swell is picking up and the seas are going to get bigger.

I used to live out here and would watch the boats on the water at night – their lights dotting the horizon and reflecting on water of the ocean. It was hard to know which was real. Reflections.

I liked that world. I miss it.

I can hear the sea lions at Simpson's reef. The south wind has brought their voice over the roar of the ocean. Simpson's reef is about five miles away, thousands of sea lions migrate there, and their barking is incessant. More noise. Could the seals manage one minute of silence?

A woman in black walks in from the beach with her dog on a pink leash. It seems as if the older women at the beach all wear black with a bit of color: varied colors of boots, mittens, hats and leashes. I wonder how a crow would look with a bit of color.

Humans take on colors, why not animals? Humans take on animals for their "bling" too: fur, teeth, leather, claws. We kill and hack animals up into pieces and eat and use their body parts for food, shelter and power. The last one is the illogical one. I don't get it. We seek the power of that which we killed. If it is power we seek - the animal's energy - wouldn't it make sense to walk in beauty with the animal, learn its lessons, and its gifts. Imagine an animal doing that to a human, killing for power. I know of Indians wanting to kill the eagle and the whale. It makes me sick. There is no need. Culture be damned! There has been enough killing and death to last an eternity. Enough lessons given that an animal does not have to die for "power." Power is within in you - it is not an external gift.

It is time for a different way.

I know, as a Comanche, I will be criticized for this belief. But the Comanche say what we believe to be true. The individual has the power. You do not take what you don't need. I read once that for the Comanche, there was no shame in divorce, or in changing your mind about going to war, or about wanting the fastest pony.

The "Indian way " has been watered-down into a mind-speak that few understand. We are not who you think we are, or want us to be, or know us to be. It isn't romantic, and all the ills of the non-Indian society are now with the Indians; shielded by the ignorance of what it means to be sovereign. Greed is the underbelly of sovereignty. I am not proud of that. But it is the truth and that is a story for another time.

A call comes in from a friend about her cat. The cat is 15 years old and has been sick. I want the cat to be okay, for the cat's sake and for my friend. She says her cat can be fixed with medication and a tail bob. It isn't the cat's

time. She will be fine. She'll just have a bit of
bling from her missing tail. I hope my friend
takes her tail back - for the cat's sake. Indian
humor.

It is 3:39.

I decide to move the car so the crows can eat.
It hurts my heart for others to go hungry. So I
move just a bit of distance but it is what they
need to feel safe. It works. The crows dance over
the granola.

The wind is stronger now and the rain
starts. The clouds lighten for a moment and the
sun, looking like the moon through the clouds,
tries its best to break through. Jailbreak. It
casts an eerie light on the ocean. And then the
heavy clouds and rain take the light away making
the day seem moodier. I think of going home, and
it makes me sad. These moody clouds also found
their way into my heart. Life off the ocean is so
different, I long for it on when I am inland.

Wanting to rush out here beyond my hour, but I
don't. I made a bargain and I don't want to be
greedy. The hour is enough. I carry it with me,
like music, joy, love, beauty, and magic.

It is 3:50.

Day Six, Sixth Hour

As I drive to the beach, I see two people
walking along Newmark Avenue. One is about nine
years old, the other looks like his grandfather.
They are holding hands and the boy breaks away to
push him up a small hill. Once they get to the
top, the boy takes his grandfather's hand again.
He didn't have to, but he did. He came back. I
like that.

My Comanche father came back, too. I was 25. He had God in his pocket then.

As I pull up to the parking lot, I see a Coast Guard boat out in the surf. They are there for two important reasons: First, to practice rescue techniques, and second, to hone their skills driving in the surf. The motor lifeboat hits a huge wave, drives up into the air to a 50-plus degree angle, pauses and then drops down. What a cowboy ride!

It is 2:17.

When I was about 13, my step-dad entered me into the Indian horse races. Back then it was a bareback race around the racetrack at the rodeo grounds. He put me on Cindy, a fast horse, and he said, "You don't weigh much, so you'll win. Hang on and kick like hell!" Winning is much better place to be when you are on a horse - no dirt clods in your face. The boat reminds me of the rush of the race. Where did I get the strength to do that? A Facebook friend remembered those days. He said I was, "fearless."

Now, I am anything but.

The wiener-dog lady is here again. Crows are calling; the sun is dripping about bits of warmth here and there mixed in with a bit of yellow. Two dogs are out playing, one barking at a stick. His human told him to stop, but the dog didn't listen. The stick talked louder.

The wiener dog lady walks by. She is dressed in black again and she has pink fingernails today. She opens the door, lets her dog in, and looks at me. She smiles. I notice that she has a dream catcher hanging from her visor. It is supposed to catch the bad dreams. I used to buy them for my kids. When your kids are afraid of the dark, it helps to give them something to believe in - small gifts to ease the dark of the night. Her bad dreams must travel with her.

I roll down the window, a five-knot wind
moves over the ocean and sand. The sky turns to a
yellow-gray. The tide is coming in, but I'll have
to check. It is hard to know if it is coming or
going. The sand is softened by the rain and wind.
What softens the human soul? Love? Hatred? Pain?
Loss?

I read a book on grief - the seminal book by
Ross. It is good. It is like a road map, showing
and explaining the various stages of grief. It
provides the five steps to healing: Denial,
Sadness, Anger, Negotiation, and Acceptance. For
some, road maps work.

But I have never traveled with a road map.

I think that in order to heal from grief,
you have to step off the road and let the journey
take you where you need to go - to trust yourself
along the way.

I think it is called faith and I think it is
how the human soul heals. I wish I had an elder

here to tell me if this is true or not. But I
don't, and so here I am, sitting at the ocean,
trying to find a way for my soul to heal. Indians
believe that when a loved one dies, half of your
soul goes with them. It is called living on the
half side. And when it is time - if ever - you
bring your soul back so that you can live again.

It is my time. I want to live.

I look out over the ocean. The clouds are
full of shapes: I see horses, a turtle, and a
frog. I once knew a man who couldn't see shapes.
He was a scientist that killed things in order to
study them. I imagined that if he could see
shapes, maybe he wouldn't need to kill.

The dog is barking again. Incessant.
Irritating. I do the practice breathing that I
just learned. I say my favorite dog's name - Oscar
for a two count, Oliver Wendell Madison Davis for
a four count. It overcomes the sharp bark of "now,

now, now!" I look out and see the problem. Another dog has stolen his stick.

There are a hundred other sticks on the beach.

My head hurts today - still. Less, but it has settled in my body, this migraine, affecting my ability to walk, with a bit of anxiety mixed in. It is like I have been rattled. I wonder if I am less patient with the dog bark because I am in pain. Is this a human condition, to be a grump when ill? I know this to be true for my husband.

I see the car next to me. It belongs to an old friend who is not a friend anymore. I suppose it is because I knew too much of what he was doing with another woman, a woman who was not his wife. He still lives his pretend life and I wonder how it is working for him. He is dressed in black and blue, and I think, perhaps, it's not so good. I feel bad for all the people that he hurt. I hoped it worked out for them. Sometimes, we excuse bad behavior because we believe that we have found a higher, better love. There is no such thing. Love is love. It comes down to what you can live with. If you choose to leave, it doesn't mean love goes away - it just changes forms - to hate, to sadness, to meanness, to loneliness, and gradually, with forgiveness, a new way of love.

I see him walking. He walks as if he is in pain. He has a young pup with him. The pup looks frightened. He walks up, puts the dog in the back of his station wagon, and wipes his feet. He walks around the side of the car, and slowly takes off his jackets. As he gets in his car, he sees me. I give him the peace sign and smile. He smiles back.

Settled.

It is 2:43.

A man in a camo jacket drives up in a big white four-wheel drive truck with big wheels and a huge cab. A woman in a Duck's jacket gets out the passenger side and they walk to the north. I don't understand the arbitrary nature of team sports. Never had. It seems like lines in the sand, and while there's money to be made and entertainment to be had - to take it to the point of a fanatical (hence, *fans*) confrontation over whether or not you are a Duck or a Beaver is ridiculous. I know...I am a woman.

Time is passing. I worry that I won't see what I need to see or learn what I need to learn and then remember, watching is just watching without expectation. If I worry or start looking, I miss the watching. And so I sit. And I watch. Perhaps this is something I should practice when I am not at the ocean, trusting that I will see and know what I need to know.

Acceptance.

I now see two Coast Guard boats on the water; both maneuvering in the high surf. I watch them point into the wave, stay true, ride up the face to the crest, hold, and then drop down the backside. The point is to stay perpendicular to the wave. If you don't, if you lose course, the boat will get swamped.

If you're not strapped-in and hang on, you will be swept overboard.

It is 2:49.

Time to feed the birds. I have cereal today. I wave my arm. Only one crow shows up. He drops down, grabs three flakes and flies off. I'm thinking that now I have a bird restaurant at the beach. I think of the thousands of birds I saw a couple days ago – the migration. It was so beautiful and I wonder about beauty. What does it mean to be beautiful? Is it a singular thing? Rare? Common? Valued? What is beauty? Will you know it when you see it, feel it, hear it, want it? Does it age? Can it become so familiar as to lose its beauty? Can it pretend? Is it youth or old age? A baby or a grandmother? And then, what if beauty becomes ugly? Is that possible?

Beauty. The simple answer is to believe all things beautiful or capable of being beautiful.

An old man wearing a hat drives up with his wife. They have fast food; I spot the typical paper wrappings. He sees the boats out on the ocean and stares. He knows boats. I can tell by his look. He glances at me and I see 'AIRBORNE' on his brim. He throws french-fries to the birds and they go crazy. He smiles and turns and looks at me. His eyes are deep-set and when he smiles, they sparkle. I wish I knew his stories and I wish I could hear him talk about the boats to his wife.

It is 2:58.

My thoughts are jumbled today. I watch the boats again. I rode in one of those boats once. They are fast and I remember feeling as if I was on ice. They are made to take the waves and they are made to survive. I think I screamed like a girl every time we hit a wave. It was fantastic.

I got sick later and it took days to get my land legs.

I look over to the man. He is pointing at the boats and talking. There is a security in knowing how something works. My step-dad could fix anything. He was fantastic with cars and even when my car broke down, could talk me through fixing it. He didn't know his gifts. I miss him in all his glory. And he was a piece of work, that man.

Three women walk out on the beach. They have two dogs, both of which are "pause and sniff" types. They sniff at everything. Done sniffing, they head out to the water's edge. One pounces and does a crab shuffle, then runs and smells and rolls. Dogs. Go figure their common way.

It is 3:08.

I am antsy. And like seeing a wave rushing towards me, I stay true and ride on to what it is.

Beth.

My Beth. She was born May 6, 1980. She was a
strong baby, always wanting to do things her way,
and grew into a woman that followed that belief.
She loved people, she loved her friends and she
loved with a capacity that to this day guides me.
No judgments, always forgiveness. She was a friend
to everyone. At her funeral, they said she was
like a comet in the sky. I long for her to be a
star, but I don't get to choose.

Beth.

There was so much more to Beth. She is more
than any words I can write. That seems trite. But
it is true. But then I think all parents feel that
way about their children. If you are a parent, you
know. I don't need to go on. If not, wait, you
will know eventually. Love is love and we all
eventually love.

So sitting here, at the ocean, watching, and wondering if God will meet his side of the bargain, I tell God what Beth is to me.

My love.

My fears.

My laughter.

My guilt.

My joy.

My shame.

My nightmare.

My peace.

My heart.

My soul.

My tears.

My anger.

My hate.

My breath.

My longing.

My immortality.

My friend.

My daughter.

My love.

Me and all of me.

How can I love and live without her? I have no answers and this is day six.

I look out over the ocean, tears in my eyes. I can't breathe. I am crying as I am watching. This watching has become my anchor in a world in which I have no understanding; where it feels as if the world has tossed me away, and without gravity, I am lost to the endless space of nothing.

Movement catches my eye. I see one dog chase another. The bigger one is slower and it doesn't take long for the first dog to catch up. She runs up ahead, grabs a stick, and brings it to him, shaking it back and forth as she trots along. He grabs it and they take off running together, passing the stick back and forth. They are two dogs that are friends under a yellow-gray sky with the roar of the ocean on an April afternoon. For today, they are this. Nothing more.

I use this. This gift of the dogs. I am here today. Watching. Nothing more. There is still a purpose to my life, no matter how small. I say my mantra, breathing, "Oscar Wendell Oliver Madison Davis." After five times, my breath returns.

I am here. It is now.

Presence.

I imagine that if I was a great thinker like Jesus or the Dali Lama or Mother Teresa, I would have found some peace by now, a new life, acceptance of Beth's passing. As if there is something wrong with me because I am not getting over the death of my daughter.

There is nothing wrong with me. None of the greater thinkers in life had children I might be wrong, but none of the ones I have read talk of their children. I am a mother whose daughter was killed. And because of that I am different, I walk different, I love different and I touch different.

I count what I see - clouds, ocean, sand, rocks, trees, beach grass, shrubs, logs, trash, four people, three dogs, a hundred seagulls and fifty or so crows.

I sit.

And beauty. I add beauty to the list.

Suddenly, the sky turns from gray to a pinkish-blue, the ocean becomes greener, the whites turn whiter, tan sand turns to purple brown, the rocks become a lighter, the beach grass

and shrubs turn a vivid green. I don't see the
people or the dogs or the birds.

I watch. Eyes forward. Aiming towards
beauty. Hanging on.

And I feel God between my falling tears.

It is 3:17.

Bastendorff Beach is about three miles from Charleston, a small fishing village living in hard times. The fishing industry, like the timber industry, has bottomed-out. As I drive over the bridge, I see an old fishing boat submerged up to its pilothouse. It is lying next to a dock, white and black with rust stains, against the blue of the bay. There are two docks by the bridge in Charleston. It's the only road out here and if an accident ever happens you have to wait until it is cleared up.

Near the dock, three sea lions are swimming under a fish processing plant. Opportunists - like Fort Indians.

I stop for bread. It is a small convenience store and I am the only one in there. A panic attack hits me as I hand her the money. The room sways and I sway. I hate anxiety, the unnamed fear with unknown and known consequences, twisting my body and mind into places that scare me. If I were aware, enlightened, blessed, would fear find me? I thank her and stumble outside and get in my car. Taking an Oscar breath, I head out to the ocean. Driving calms me. Always has.

I drive up to the beach, bucking against a headwind from the south, the analogy obvious.

It is 1:33.

A storm is blowing through today. There are "sheep in the pasture," an old sailing term used to describe white caps on the water. It means the wind is about 20 to 25 knots. I remember the first time I saw wind on the ocean, the first time I sailed, it felt like I was moving to God's breath. It comes as close to the feeling you get as a kid when you are moving back and forth on a huge rope swing only to eventually let go and fly off into the lake. But sailing is better, much better because the flying part lasts.

I look out over the ocean - the waves are struggling against the wind, their tops blowing to the north in a swirl of white. The ocean seems to be making friends with the wind, perhaps to learn its secret.

"Imagine what we could do together," it whispers.

My car is moving in the wind, a gust comes around every so often, and my pen shakes on the paper. The rain is coming down at a slant. I ignore the wipers today; the wind is doing a fine job moving the rain off the windshield.

Sand is taking on the wind, huge eddies swirl by. The beach is changing; small sand dunes are forming against logs and rocks. Down by the river, seagulls are huddled down. They are not moving, not eating. They are just waiting. Clouds hide the sun, and yet, every once in awhile, you can sense the sun's possibility.

It is a light gray day with a wind that wants to win.

A red truck is here. My Comanche dad had a red truck. Towards the end of his life, he drove it to church on Sundays, and to Bible study meetings on Wednesday. He said God made him a Deacon, him, a puny Indian. I remember riding with him, sitting in the backseat and watching his head. He had on a baseball cap that said, "Red Power." He used to run red lights saying, "Red is for Indians!"

This is the last day of my bargain with God. I am here with the third day of a migraine and am angry that this pain is clouding the time I spend out here. I don't know what I anticipate from today, but last night I dreamed that I was Queen Elizabeth and the cool part was that I was excited at all the things I would be able to do for others as Queen. No more poverty or ignorance, medical care for all. In the dream, I was floating in a beautiful white dress and I couldn't wait to get started helping others.

A seagull blasts by, riding the wind. I look out over the ocean and see two more, one taking something from the beach, taking flight merely by holding its wings up, catching the wind, only to be blown backwards up to the sky, drop the something, and then follow it down to the sand. Over and over it does this while the other seagull, staying on the sand, hops after it.

I don't think I have ever seen a bird fly backwards.

More join in and one runs into the wind only to be pulled back, and flies off to the north. I can feel the wind as it moves them. And now I can say that I have seen many birds fly backwards.

Sanity might question my perception.

More seagulls come and they fly over me, some hovering in suspension against the wind. They are still. Then the sand blows over them and the beach looks like a sand storm. And they fly away.

Everything is different when the wind blows strong.

What would it feel like to ride the wind? Ride the storms?

And then hundreds of seagulls fly back in. I don't see where they came from, they just are. All riding the wind, swooping up, darting to the left or right, down, then up, a few seem to fly upside down, and a few, letting go, fly backwards with the wind.

I grab the bread and start throwing it out. There aren't any people here today and the birds are hungry. But they're always hungry. They rush the car, fighting for the bread, stealing it away only to be chased down. There is no enjoyment, only a feeding frenzy. Three crows fight over a slice of bread; black feathers flying in the wind. The wind catches one of them, its wings out to be taken up into the sky in flight. He arcs backwards

and tries to return only to be blown about 20 feet
down the beach.

I look to my left and see a crow biting a rock.
Odd. I doubt there are any bugs under the rock.
Maybe this one, this crow, is a bit off, thinking
a rock is food. I don't imagine it makes him any
less hungry though.

Three girls walk out on the beach, their hair
blowing wildly in the wind; one in a pink jacket,
another in a blue jacket and the other in a black
jacket. Pink Jacket jumps on Blue Jacket's back.
They walk piggyback-style for about 100 feet and
then Pink Jacket jumps off and hugs Blue Jacket. I
wonder if they are friends or related? They stop
to write in the sand. They walk, they play, and
they push each other towards the water.

They kneel down and draw in the sand.

Beth was an artist. Since she was young, she
drew and painted all the time. I think what she
drew was what she loved and she gave the pictures

to her friends. She drew animals. In high school, she bloomed as an artist. She had an amazing art teacher whose encouragement took Beth to new levels. I have book and books of her art. I still have all her art supplies. Even still. Even now.

Art. Art was Beth's choice. I encouraged my kids to have a passion. My oldest chose surfing, my next, guitar, Beth, art and the youngest, well, it started out with video games, but now it is words. Beth won contests and I don't think she ever knew how good she was. No matter what her teachers said, her friends or her family, she seemed small to it. I wonder if I could have done more for her.

Regret.

Every year on her birthday, I take a piece of her art and have it enlarged to a poster-sized print and send copies out to the family. I have a beautiful piece she did of frogs. She loved frogs. We used to sing Three Dog Night's, "Jeremiah was a

Bullfrog, was a good friend of mine!" at the top of our lungs. After she passed, I had a bullfrog personalized license plate; people gave me hundreds of frog cards and figurines. After ten years, I am worn out from bullfrogs. I don't seek them out anymore as a symbol of Beth.

Beth was tough - from snowboarding to wakeboarding to skateboarding - she kept up with her brothers. Nothing ever hurt and she never complained. She used to give piggyback-rides to her brothers, saying she was strong enough.

When I see girls, I see Beth.

I have been carrying the loss of Beth for ten years. My grandson, when he hurts himself, hides the scratch or cut. He doesn't show anyone. I'm like that too, it's just this pain I hide isn't physical - it is spiritual. I am tired. It is time to let go of the pain, to show it, so that maybe I can heal.

It is why I made the bargain.

It is 1:48.

It seems to me, that if given the chance, the wind today could take it all. Nature can be extreme. Left unchecked, I wonder what nature would do. Would flowers grow wherever? Are we the cultivators of the nature? I have a friend who loves to garden, he read somewhere that humans were here solely to tend to the plants. I wish we lived in a world that honored the earth a bit more, tended to it a bit more. But we don't, we live in a world where pollution takes our air and water, and war spreads like a disease.

I wonder if nature can forgive the human touch?

I wonder about God and whether or not he likes what he has created and what creation has become. I think of the seagulls, greedy for food, not unlike humans or animals. Even plants are greedy, given the opportunity: One species can wipe out another. What is this need for more? To take? To endlessly, endlessly take?

I see a seagull off to my left. He is standing on the sand by my car. Red feet, black toe nails, black spec on its beak, white feathers painted with tattooed grays and browns, he looks like a punk rocker. My other grandson likes to do his hair like that. He takes the mike and sings like the best of them. He is only 10.

Crows, well, crows are the country western singers.

I wonder what I look like these days. What has grief done to me?

The girls are still out playing, and I roll down my window. Sand blasts my face and finds its way into my eyes. Rubbing my eyes, I roll up the window.

With the wind helping it along, I wonder where the sand would go today if given a choice.

My car is hit by a gust of wind. I have been out here with the storms many times. The seas get big, the waves crash, trees moan, animals hide,

and it can become a bit wild. It isn't like a
Wyoming storm, where you see it building out over
the mountains only to blow through and leave. On
the coast, the storms hit hard and fast and they
do damage, snap power lines, down trees, or cause
flash flooding.

And yet, when in a storm, I feel safe. Like
being in the eye of the storm.

Perception.

I think of the need for humans to want to be
immortal. I wonder what death is doing to Beth. My
mother would tell me to look to religion. My
Comanche father and brother would tell me that I
am strong and that God is with me. My step-dad
would smile and go to the fridge and take out a
beer, light a cigarette and turn on the
television.

I think, for me, if God is Chicago, it doesn't
matter how you get there. When I learned of how my
daughter died, two years after the accident, based

upon an Expert's Accident Reconstruction Opinion,
three experts, actually, I was in Chicago. I don't
think it was a coincidence. For two years we
didn't know how she officially died. It was
speculation that she was driving the motorcycle,
the boy she was with - the one who lived - said he
wasn't driving. The expert disagreed. No one asked
me. I know my daughter. She didn't know how to
drive a motorcycle, never had, never did.

When I read of kidnappings, I ache for the
parents who live every day without knowing. I
think that as parents, we need to know,
regardless.

A friend calls. She has been fighting for her
job and I have been along for the ride. I hope it
is good news. I take the call because I believe
that is part of why I am here - to help. She has
news and eventually it will be good. She unwound
the problem, got the answers and will be putting
it all together in a couple of weeks. I call her
Johnny Red Feather. She needed an Indian name

because she is the last of her family; her parents and her husband all passed within the last couple of years.

It is 1:59.

A man drives up in a Jeep Cherokee Laredo. I smile because it is red, and Cherokee Laredo is just another way to say Indian Cowboy. Not my tribe, but close enough. He is older, a bit heavy, large glasses, and has a square head. He is missing some hair and he reminds me of someone I once feared. I don't want to have anything to do with him. Not based upon him, but upon my perceptions.

That isn't fair.

My dark anxiety kicks in: Don't trust, don't look, leave, run, run, run! But I don't. I have a bargain with God - to watch and to be here. And so I stay and fidget. I think that the wind and I have a lot in common; choosing to run when the weather turns dark. But the bargain gives me strength.

I stay.

I look over at him. He is now reading the Bible. I can tell because it's a black book with thin paper. He has it in one hand, the other he uses to point at the words as he reads.

The Bible? Here at the ocean? Well, now, isn't that an ironic turn to this journey. It is ironic because I was raised with the Bible, my mother and step-grandmother took me to a revival when I was 12, and I "found" Jesus. You should have seen their eyes – so proud I found The Way. I used to sing Christian songs with my step-grandmother, she on the piano, "Oh What a Friend We Have in Jesus." My mom hadn't sung in years.

My goodness.

I let that "founding" go years ago. For good reasons. When Beth was nine years old, I was in the middle of a custody battle with their father.

It was horrible and it was ugly. One night, I took a walk and talked with God. I gave him my children to care for. We had a deal.

God forgot. Beth was killed.

And now this? The Bible? Come on, God, don't you have something better to show me? Really? An old man in a red Jeep Cherokee Laredo? Really? Really? I pause. And I think, "I DON'T WANT THE BIBLE TO BE THE MESSAGE!" Back to that? Really?

I look to the other truck. It is a Ram Charger. Great. I am a Capricorn. The Ram. The Goat. Whatever. Corny, corny, corny. I am seeing too much of the weird. Hunter Thompson said, "When the going gets weird, the weird turn pro."

I am now a Pro.

I look out over the ocean, the clouds are easing. The wind is lightening up. The "Jacket Girls" head back to their car. I think of my Indian father, how the Bible saved him from alcohol. How he could sing Amazing Grace in

Comanche. How his eyes lit up when he talked about being a man of God. I think of my Mom, going to church every Sunday, praying for her family and friends.

Okay. Fine. For you, Dad. And you, Mom. So I can tell you that I tried.

I peek over. The guy was still reading the Bible. My anxiety is on high alert, but I hear a whisper, "In order to live, you must step outside of your life, be curious, step around your fear. You have to fight through fear because to do otherwise, you become the fear."

That was a long whisper. The last time I heard the whisper that long was when I was four years old. Some wild horses were stampeding and I was in the direct path of the horses. This whisper said, "Pretend you are a rock. The horses won't step on a rock." I did and they didn't.

I roll down my window.

The man sees me do this and I make the motion for him to roll down his window. He fumbles with the Bible, sets it down and rolls his window down.

I smile and ask him what passage he is reading. He looks down and then back to me and says, "Jeremiah."

"Which chapter?" I ask.

"Chapter 30. Why?" he asks.

And then I let it go. "I am here looking for answers to my daughter's passing. I saw you reading the Bible and thought I would ask."

"Just a minute," he says. And he gets out and comes over to my car. I feel as if the pelican has just gotten too close.

"My name is Ty," I said, and reached out to shake his hand.

"Jay," he said.

While he was speaking, two cars pull up: a black one and a white one. Funny, I thought. Another "Pro moment."

"What do you believe about death?" he asked.

What a question.

"Where do you believe your daughter to be?"

Another.

"Do you believe in Heaven?"

And yet another.

I said, "I feel her all the time. Yesterday, I cried, and felt God through my tears."

"Jesus cried for Lazarus and then resurrected him."

"I know that passage," I said.

"Do you believe in Heaven?" he asked.

"Not heaven, but another place of existence," I said.

"We don't believe in Hell, but for us, your daughter is in "Shell," the common grave of mankind waiting for resurrection," he said.

I thought to myself, "Oh my, what can of worms did I open?" Crap.

"Your daughter is asleep waiting for Jesus to resurrect her."

I deflect. "Do you go to church?"

"My wife used to be Catholic and then she got tired of the lies, I'm a Jehovah's Witness now. She is too."

"Your religion has quite a reputation," I said. I smile as I say this and he looks up and chuckles.

"Did your wife pass?" I asked.

"No, no, she is my second wife."

"I asked because you said your wife in the past tense."

"My first wife was from another country looking for a way to the States; her love for me was only for getting here. I was optimistic and took what I could at that time. Don't think I would now."

I pause.

"Look, Jay," I said. "I believe that if God is Chicago, it doesn't matter how you get there – just that you do."

"That's fine, that's fine. That's a good start. Let me get some brochures. My goodness, we knock on doors in neighborhoods all the time just to find someone like you. Hold on, I have them in my Jeep."

Just like me? What is that? Or rather, who is that? I wait and watch the ocean. Clouds are dancing and I see shapes in them. But I am not looking to name them. I just watch them. A dog runs up to a black car, the owner is in a bright-red coat and the dog has on a matching color.

He comes back with about ten Watchtower brochures. He thumbs through them, and I stop him.

"How about this one, it talks about God's New World," I said.

"Sure, sure."

"And I can go online to read other stuff?" I asked.

"Yes, yes. That will work."

I tell him about the seventh day and the seventh hour and my promise - my bargain with God.

"Ah, like Churchill," he says. "The invasion of Normandy."

"I'll read about that," I say.

"I spent 20 years in the military," he said.

I didn't know what to say.

"Back then, if someone asked me about Jeremiah, I would have started singing, 'Jeremiah was a Bullfrog!'"

And he started singing it.

On the seventh day of the seventh hour, Beth spoke to me. I know that I didn't have any expectations about this bargain, but I never thought I would learn of healing and immortality from an old military man, reading the Bible at the ocean; a man who drove a red Jeep named after an Indian cowboy, singing, "Jeremiah was a Bullfrog!"

God has a sense of humor. I think I like it.

It is 2:33.

"For I will restore health to you, And your wounds I will heal," declares the Lord. - Jeremiah 30:17

Epilogue

My seven days and seven hours occurred on April 13 to 19, 2012. In the ten years since my daughter passed, I have sought to find peace. I have written music, talked to counselors, ministers, sat with friends, written journals, and read books. These things and people took me close, but grief always came back around, through a memory, a death day, a birthday, or holidays; then it was the 100th floor again, and I became lost to the pain as if she had just died.

The idea to sit with nature came to me on a drive back from the ocean. It was on the 10th anniversary of Beth's passing. I didn't have any expectations as to what I would do or see or what I may find. I just thought that if I sat at the ocean for an hour for seven days, something in me could change. Seven is a sacred number after all.

It changed my life.

I believe two things now: First, is that grief cannot be healed with the human touch, because before there were humans, there was nature. I don't think it matters where you go, just that you go to a place outside of the human influence. Humans have such a heavy hand on the world. Second, God listens. It doesn't matter what you call him. What matters is that you believe because it is this belief that will guide you through the dark nights.

I certainly didn't think this journey would end up in this way. It took me by surprise. And even when it was sitting in front of me, I wanted something different. It took Jay singing to me to change my heart, to open my soul.

As I write this, when I think of grief and pain, I now think of the ocean - its endless movement where nothing stays and nothing leaves. It is my symbol that I prayed for strength. It is my healing touch.

God listened and God stayed until I heard back. And God delivered more: On the seventh day of the seventh hour of my bargain with God, God brought me Beth. I thought he forgot his promise to me – the promise I made when she was nine. He didn't. He made sure she was in his care. Even now. Even in this way.

Perhaps, if you need to find a way with grief, seven hours at the ocean may help. But you don't have to go to the ocean. You can go anywhere – the mountains, the park, a river, your backyard or balcony – just to watch. Let me know what comes….

ABOUT THE AUTHOR

Born in California, transplanted to Wyoming, only to end up living on the edge of the world - the Southern Oregon coast. A mother, lawyer, judge, Comanche, writer, painter, and singer songwriter, Ty is still learning what it means to be a human being.

12949163R00064

Made in the USA
Charleston, SC
07 June 2012